THE RULES OF DECENCY

Carol Pemrich Hauser

Fulton Books
Meadville, PA

Published by Fulton Books 2024

ISBN 979-8-89427-522-2 (paperback)
ISBN 979-8-89427-523-9 (digital)

Printed in the United States of America

To my brother, Glen William Pemrich
(August 24, 1961 to April 11, 2015)
The most decent human being I have ever known.

PREFACE

I wrote this book because of the below meme I saw on Facebook. It started out as a short article, but as I wrote and talked with other people, I realized the need to expand on each element. What used to be referred to as common decency is getting lost in our society. We are not teaching everyone what it takes to be decent. These basic and most important concepts are what make us humans the very best we can be.

It costs $0.00
to be a decent
human being.

As I considered the meaning of this meme, I wondered why people equate money with being decent, and I concluded that it doesn't equate. Being poor is not a prerequisite for being a decent human being. I wonder why we must be reminded to be decent and conclude that maybe people just don't know how.

Decency 101 isn't a class you take in college. I think some of us are lucky enough to have a family to teach us decency as we grow up. Maybe it's something we learned in church or in bits and pieces to rectify the mistakes we made, but if we don't learn in youth, we carry this lack of decency into adulthood with no small repercussions.

Being a decent human being isn't always easy, but it *is* worthwhile. Here's how.

BE GENUINE!

Be yourself, no matter if you are a confident socialite or a computer nerd. Not only will you be a happier person, but people will find it easier to relate to you. You are great just the way you are, so just be yourself.

I learned to be genuine in my forties. I never understood why so many people did not like me, but now I know it's because they couldn't tell who I was. How could they when I didn't know myself? It took so long because, as I grew up, I was never allowed to find out. Growing up as the fifth of eight kids to an alcoholic father and a narcissist mother, I only knew who I wasn't. I believed I was useless, I couldn't do anything right, my hair was miserable, I was an ugly little pig who was only good for kicking around, literally. I tried so hard to be worthy, to be good enough for my parents to love. They died before I could resolve that in my head.

Part of why I didn't know who I was is because I was not allowed to make simple everyday decisions, even about what clothes I wore. I rarely had new clothes, and when I did, my mother bought things for me when I wasn't with her. The clothes I had to wear made me a laughingstock at school. Tops didn't fit right, and pants were out of style. My mother had abysmal fashion sense, and one day she bought me a pantsuit that had white pants. I hated those white pants, and I told her, but she forced me to wear them to a party at some friend's house. I went into the bathroom and purposely ripped a hole in the white pants so I didn't have to wear them. I put on some jeans I had sneaked in.

I could tell how angry my mom was by her pursed lips and pointed stare. That night at home, she screamed at me about the pants and how much money they had cost. I had some money from babysitting, so I tossed it at her and told her I owned those pants now and would never wear them. I then went upstairs, opened the bathroom medicine cabinet, and proceeded to swallow every single pill I found. Then I told my mother. She called the doctor, who told her to make me throw up. Most parents have ipecac at home for this, but not my mom. She made me drink dish soap and forced me to until I threw up, then she took me to the hospital, where I stayed for three days. I didn't want to go home, but they wouldn't let me stay.

After that incident, I pretended to be other people, like my best friend Cindy. Cindy lived around the corner from me, and I used to see her walking her beautiful Alaskan Malamute dogs. I admired her easy, confident mannerisms and the way she stood up for herself. When anyone said anything negative about her, she would look them right in the eye and tell them exactly how and why they were wrong. I could never do that, so I tried to act like Cindy. But mostly, I hid from my own family at her house as much as possible. She was like a second sister to me. I had a silly attraction to her oldest brother, Jesse. Jesse was one of those golden boys every girl fawns over, and he knew it. But it was the other brother, Clarence, for whom I really fell. Clarence was quiet like me and every bit as handsome. The shy way he tried to hide his teenage acne endeared him to me. We would stare at each other across the room, and silently, we cared for each other. We only talked about our feelings twice, and nothing ever came of it. I rarely talk with Cindy these days. We grew apart as people do, but she was important to me. In many ways, she saved my life, and I will always call her a friend. Clarence got married, and I think he still lives in Milwaukee. I will always call him a friend too.

I pretended to be other people I admired as well. My friend Sandy, whom I luckily befriended on the first day of high school, was one of them. Sandy protected underdogs, including me, from the mean kids. Two others I pretended to be were Erica Kane from *All My Children* and Marcia Brady from *The Brady Bunch*. Erica Kane was tough as nails and always got what she wanted, and Marcia Brady was so pretty and popular. I wanted to be like them—someone other people liked and respected and wanted to be around. They portrayed the strength and confidence I didn't have. When they talked, people listened. When I pretended to be like them, I felt stronger and better, but that deception was only skin-deep. I was a mental wreck inside, and it didn't take much for my true colors to show through. I was exhausted, and I hated myself so much that I wished I were dead.

I thought if I could be like Cindy or Sandy, nobody could really hurt me. I didn't understand that by trying to be someone else, I was trying, in vain, to get my parents, some boy, or anyone else to love me. It never happened, and finally, I gave up trying. Then suddenly, as if by magic, other people started to like me. I was shocked and surprised by this, and it took me a while to trust it. Not everybody likes me, of course, but enough of them for me to see that when I am being my true, genuine self, people notice, and I don't even have to try. It just happens.

I love who I am now. I am strong and mostly confident. I am far from perfect, but I stand up for myself and others. I am kind and helpful. I strive to keep good relationships with those I love. I am a great writer and a fun person to be silly with. I have the most fun throwing pillows and marshmallows with my grandkids. I am a good friend and a fighter against evil and injustice. I am too fat, but I am pretty, and I love to laugh. I can honestly say that I love myself, and that's what we should all strive for. Being genuine means loving yourself for everything you are and all that you are not.

We are not meant to be perfect, and it is a waste of time and energy, especially if you are trying to be perfect for someone else. We waste so much time trying to please others. If someone else can't love you for exactly who you are, let them go. I was not allowed to be myself as a child, so it took me a very long time to discover who I am as an adult. I tried to be what I thought my parents wanted me to be. The trouble was that they didn't want a child named Carol; they wanted a robotic maid, and a silent one at that. I was always quiet because speaking up as a child meant being bullied and bruised both inside and out. Now that I have given up trying to be someone else, I can be my own genuine self, and my own opinion of me is all that matters. Now instead of bruises, I have laugh lines, and many other people like me. But if they don't, it doesn't bother me. Their opinion of me is none of my business.

RESPECT YOURSELF!

Nobody will respect you if you don't respect yourself.

Many of us have self-esteem issues and have been traumatized by past experiences. Many of us need therapy, suffer from depression, and take medication for anxiety. I am one of these people, so I need a reminder to respect myself. A lack of self-respect will stop us from getting help when we need it and make us feel even worse when bad things happen.

I am discovering this lack of self-respect in myself just as I am writing about it here. It is ugly to me. It seems shameful and inconceivable, and yet here I am learning that I have to respect myself before others will show me that same respect. I have repeating patterns of impulsivity, which manifest negatively in my finances. Because of my own lack of self-respect, I have experienced serious debt, bankruptcy, and homelessness.

My daughter has trouble speaking up at work and often feels frustrated and disheartened. She is afraid others will feel badly if she has to tell them what to do. A friend of mine bravely revealed her gambling addiction. I have so much respect for both my daughter and my friend for their wonderful countenances and for trusting me with their difficult challenges, but it is hard for me to watch them struggle.

A notable example of this lack of self-respect is seen on the TV show *Hoarders*. These sad people have filled their homes and lives with so much stuff that it has become a handicap that needs professional intervention. The whole scope of living in a non-self-respectful way is seen in these shows.

Hoarding is an extreme manifestation of living with a lack of self-respect. Most of these folks can pinpoint a cause or occurrence, such as divorce, a death, or some other large stressor, as the time when the hoarding began. I wonder, if they had sought out help in dealing with these difficult matters right away, would they have been able to avoid the conditions they find themselves living in?[1]

---

[1] Anything mentioned in this chapter as "behavior" is not meant to demean or offend those suffering from actual mental illness.

Oftentimes we don't seek out help because it is uncomfortable to have our shortcomings brought into the focus of our own accountability or offered up to the potential for judgment by others. There is a social stigma surrounding getting mental or other help, and we can get caught between being stigmatized by our behavior and going to see a therapist. When I first started looking for a daily money manager, I happened upon a blog of people who were extremely judgmental of those struggling to get help organizing and paying bills. Reading their comments made me feel embarrassed and shameful. Those bloggers saw my lack of self-respect as a character flaw and not a changeable pattern of behavior, and they certainly did not applaud the bravery of actively seeking much-needed help.

Some of these behaviors have been unjustly classified as "character flaws." However, character flaws, like sociopathy, cannot recognize respect, neither for themselves nor anyone else. In his book *The People of the Lie*,[2] M. Scott Peck has thoroughly discussed these character flaws and tentatively labeled them as evil. Evil is being researched by Mr. Peck and others, and from what I can gather, it is something innate

---

[2] M. Scott Peck, *People of the Lie* (Simon and Schuster Touchstone Press, 1983).

and unchangeable. We should not condemn a lack of self-respect because respect can be recognized, and anyone can be taught to recognize it and learn its potential for growth in self-discovery, as opposed to the evils inherent and unchangeable in a character flaw.

Let's not take this to mean we won't have moments of weakness and vulnerability. Those are going to happen. In fact, they must, for us to recognize them and experience personal growth in overcoming them. The harm our lack of self-respect does is in NOT being able to recognize those moments for what they truly are and in NOT using them for personal growth.

I can get so mired down in weak moments that I take no action either way. It's embarrassing for me to continually use credit poorly, but it is equally embarrassing to ask for help. That is the lack of self-respect talking. That voice tells me I am just weak, that I am stupid to let this bother me so much, and that it is shameful to have this problem in the first place. This is the voice I must squelch because if I don't get help or take extra measures of self-discipline to counteract the bad behaviors, I let my own disrespect run over me.

How can we be sure we are suffering from a lack of self-respect? Consider these questions: Do others get tired of hearing you talk about the same issues? Do they roll their eyes? Are you in a constant state of anxiety and seem stuck and incapable of finding good solutions to your problems? Do you discover these same problems wherever you go, even if you move to another home, get a new job, or get out of a relationship? Do you feel shame or embarrassment over this issue? That is a lack of self-respect, and it can manifest as anger, self-pity, addiction, depression, violence, and suicide. This can seem like a plague that follows you everywhere you go and can wreak havoc on you at every moment.

Sometimes we have to unlearn things about ourselves in childhood. When you go through life never experiencing respect from others, you learn not to respect yourself. It's easy to fall into repeating patterns of behavior, such as using a credit card needlessly or staying in a job in which you feel miserable. In fact, realizing you suffer from a lack of self-respect can make you feel even more miserable at first, but it can easily turn into hope. All it takes to turn that around is to make a conscious decision to respect yourself. By choosing self-respect first and foremost, you can make better decisions with better outcomes.

Choosing to respect yourself is a basic concept of being a decent human being, but it takes practice and active thought. If I didn't care about being in debt, I wouldn't have to make a change, but because the consequences of debt or bankruptcy are unacceptable to me, I have contacted a personal money manager to assist me in getting my financial situation under control so I can move forward with confidence and self-respect.

My friend has gone into local casinos and purposely had herself banished from them. I applaud her bravery in doing that. It showed her self-respect, and I believe she can continue on her path to recover her shining self-respect. She is a beautiful person with much capacity for caring and love.

My daughter is finding her own path. I feel that she learned her lack of self-respect from me while I raised her. While it is not a major problem, she may have to unlearn that and some other things. I see that some of the discrepancies of my own childhood have affected my children. So many times I felt dispirited by the things I could not give them, such as good self-esteem or self-respect, because I did not have those things myself. I can only acknowledge my shortcomings, ask their forgiveness, and encourage them to seek out ways to effectively overcome these issues in their lives.

Taking accountability for my actions is what I need to do. Every action has consequences, and when I act out of self-respect, the consequences are positive, and I am no longer stuck in a loop of negativity. Holding myself accountable is something any decent, self-respecting person would do.

TELL THE TRUTH!

Honesty is a cornerstone of decency. Being honest about your intentions, expectations, and boundaries makes every encounter you have stronger and more positive. Honesty is a tool for building trust and respect, but dishonesty, even in small amounts, creates confusion and misunderstanding.

I once dated a man who was completely incapable of telling the truth. I will call him John. John would tell me he couldn't see me, then show up at my door. He would say he wanted to break up with me, then tell me he couldn't live without me. He lied about absolutely everything, from where he lived to what he ate for breakfast. His lies left me confused and frustrated because they were so unnecessary. I believe John is a pathological liar who is also a sociopath.

Sociopaths make everyone they come in contact with liars. We believe what they tell us and, in doing so, we pass on their lies and become liars ourselves.

Normal people cannot understand sociopaths, but actually, they are telling their own truths. It is up to us to recognize a lie from a sociopath, then disassociate ourselves from them. In his book, *People of the Lie*, M. Scott Peck goes into great detail about sociopathy and how it causes chaos and angst in the lives of everyone around them.

We only have to turn on our television or open a magazine to see how dishonesty tries to continually win us over. Buy this car, and you will be wildly successful and popular. Wear these jeans, and no matter what size your hips are, you will suddenly be slender. Dishonesty is a driving force in marketing, and there are shysters everywhere trying to get something from our money to our very identity. We don't like to be lied to, so we must be constantly aware and not fall victim to deceit around us every day.

Here is a quote from the website of The (Dis) honesty Project[3].

> From plagiarism, to infidelity, to financial fraud, dishonesty seems to be a universal part of the world we live in. Going far beyond

---

[3] Dan Ariely and Yael Melamed, The (Dis) Honesty Project, http://thedishonestyproject.com/film/.

scandalous headlines, cheating isn't just happening on a news-worthy scale, it's happening in small ways everywhere. It's human nature to lie, we all do it! But little fibs can snowball into large-scale problems with major implications for society. We don't really under-stand the causes and complexi-ties of dishonesty, but reminding ourselves about our own morality makes us behave better.

There are two good ways to discern if someone is lying. First, if you ask a question that only requires a yes or no answer and get anything but yes or no, they are lying. Liars need time to make up a story, so they preface it with extra words first. Second, if what someone tells you is confusing and they cannot or will not offer a plausible explanation, they are probably lying. The truth is plain, clear, and without ambiguity.

We have a choice in what we believe, and our beliefs become our standards of decency, morality, and righteousness. They are unique to each of us. Do you believe in strict adherence to Bible teachings or cultural norms without options for individuality? Do you believe in free thinking, spontaneity, and reincarnation? Each of us has our own truths, which can be altered and evolved as we move through different stages of our lives.

Our truths stem from our beliefs, and as we develop through our lives, we must examine our beliefs and adjust them. Some people never waiver from the truths they learned as children, regardless of evidence of their fallibility. But even in this inability or unwillingness to change, living in your truth and staying on its course makes one a decent human being unless that truth is hurtful or hate-filled, and living in those truths has its consequences.

In his book *The Code of the Extraordinary Mind*,"[4] Vishen Lakhiani talks about living within socially acceptable norms. The things we were taught in childhood, which we question because they no longer make sense to us or serve the same purpose, the author calls bullshit rules, or "Brules." They are the rules people and societies make up as ways to control us and make life orderly, such as speed limits and religious dogma.

"Brules" have a place in our world because they keep us safe or help make life meaningful. But if we

---

[4]   Vishen Lakhiani, founder of MindValley, *The Code of the Extraordinary Mind*, e-book format.

choose to go against those rules or laws, there are consequences. Sometimes the consequences are hard and negative, and sometimes they are inspirational and positive. We have to decide for ourselves what truths we will conform to. And in accepting our truths, we also accept the consequences.

Each truth has a consequence, and sometimes a negative consequence is what keeps us from telling the truth. An example is when a child eats a cookie before dinner and is confronted. That child will probably lie about eating the cookie despite obvious evidence, such as crumbs and chocolate on their face. It's not the lie the child fears; it is the consequences. Punishment, shame, and other consequences are unpleasant. We avoid the uncomfortable, unpleasant consequences by lying.

So why should we ever tell the truth? It comes down to asking what kind of person we want to be. We need not strive for perfection, but *I* want to be able to hold my head up high and not be embarrassed or ashamed of who I am, so I choose to tell the truth and accept those consequences, and if I no longer believe those truths, I can change what I believe to better reflect who I want to be. As long as I am honest with myself and the people around me, I have a much better grasp at decency.

LISTEN!

Following the chapter on telling the truth with one on listening seems essential. Would we be eager to speak our truths if we were not being listened to?

Listening is a skill that takes patience, practice, and desire, but it's also easy to learn. The simplest model I have found is in an article from Karyn K. MacRae,[5] IOM, CAE, CMP, US Chamber of Commerce Foundation. In Communication 101: Listening for Dummies, Ms. MacRae states three simple elements for effective listening.

- *Focus.* Tune out all outside distractions. Turn away from your computer screen, put

---

[5] Karyn K. MacRae, IOM, CAE, CMP, US Chamber of Commerce Foundation, Communication 101: Listening for Dummies, Ms. MacRae, January 15, 2015, http://institute.uschamber.com/communication-101-listening-for-dummies/.

your phone down, and give 100 percent of your attention to the person to whom you are listening. Maintaining eye contact is also a key element. Establishing and maintaining eye contact shows someone you respect them and care about what they are trying to say.

- *Relax.* This is most applicable when you're on the receiving end of a complaint, criticism, or something negative. It's human nature to tense up and go on the defensive, but if you're able to relax, you're much more likely to listen to what is actually being said.
- *Process.* Before responding with a knee-jerk reaction, take time to consider your response. It's okay to follow up if you don't have the answer right away.

Everything in nature requires communication, and listening is part of the process of effective communication. Even a newborn child will scream at the top of its lungs to get attention. What happens when that child is not heard? He/She gets angry and yells even louder.

Why is it that we sometimes have to yell at the top of our lungs to get someone to listen to us? We hear because our ears process sound. It's human nature to pay attention to loud sounds, and it's instinctual to want loud, annoying sounds to stop. Washington, DC, is a mecca of very loud lobbyists, and they wear down politicians with their unrelenting persistence. But when someone is quiet, we may ignore them or form a false belief that they have nothing to say, so we don't listen.

Think of a time when you tried to talk to someone who refused to listen. I remember vividly the day I decided to divorce my first husband. I needed to tell him something, but he would not listen. I stood there in tears, trying to speak, while he went about his work. He never turned to look at me and kept brushing me aside with platitudes. I don't know if he realized that it was the moment he lost me. If he had just stopped working and looked at me, even for a minute, who knows? We might still be married. We can become angry and defensive or feel isolated and despondent if we are not heard. We see the effects of this in divorce courts, principal's offices, bars, therapy, or even in the news. Our actions have to be seen because our voices are not heard.

Every encounter we have with another person is an opportunity to create goodwill, respect, and trust, but if neglected, the damage can be serious. Just this morning, I contacted our mortgage company, and I had to tell the customer service representative who I was three times. Two of those were because he asked me if I was Mr. Hauser. Obviously, he was not listening. I have had other experiences with companies where I felt I was not heard. I have closed accounts and refused to shop, and I have told others about negative interactions. Good businesses understand this and train their employees to do more listening than talking.

I believe if we could and would take time to truly listen to each other, we would avoid most of the problems we encounter in life. The relief and release we feel when we have truly been listened to are cathartic. I was raised Catholic and recall, even as a child, how I felt when I confessed my innermost thoughts to a priest. I was just a little kid, and that man did nothing but listen to me. He didn't even know who I was, but I did feel good afterward! Someone listened!

We don't have to become priests, lobbyists, or therapists in order to make a positive impact on another person; we just have to stop for a moment and let them speak. Then we need to listen!

ASK!

I don't like to ask for things. That's just who I am, and it is very hard for me to do so. Growing up as a highly sensitive kid with all of the chaos and violence in my home, it was much better to sit in the corner and hope nobody saw me. I was usually very quiet because speaking up could mean getting into all kinds of trouble. Plus, in my home, nine times out of ten, the answer would be no, so I learned not to ask for anything.

Sometimes, I will do something impulsively without asking. I took my grandchildren for haircuts once, which caused hard feelings. If I had asked and been told no, my grandkids would have had bushy hair, but I might have learned that others have boundaries I should not cross unless I ask.

I had to include this chapter *because* I don't like to ask, but asking is a major part of honesty, listening, and having self-respect. It is a good reminder for me. It causes me to step out of my own comfort zone, but it also has to do with establishing trustworthiness and reliability from another's perspective.

Denial and rejection are why it is hard to ask. We put ourselves in a vulnerable position and bend to the will of someone else. If we are gracious and accept the rejection, it shows others that we are mature and trustworthy. That does not mean we can't or shouldn't ask more questions in order to gain a better understanding or try to convince them, but anger and refusal to accept a "no" are childish and will make it more difficult for others to approach us for any reason in the future.

Sometimes I hate to ask because the process is frustrating. There are those who have to have a committee meeting to see if the request is feasible and warranted. People like me who are results-oriented lose patience with processes and procedures. If I have deemed it feasible and warranted, I just do it and accept the consequences. I once took my small teen Sunday school class to a local doughnut shop for class without asking and had angry exchanges with the parents and the pastor afterward. I was not happy with those consequences, but I learned a valuable lesson about asking (at least about doughnuts on Sunday).

I am learning to ask for specific things in my role as caregiver to my husband, who suffers from Alzheimer's disease. We caregivers do so much giving and caring that we hardly stop to give a second thought to how someone else can help us. We are just out there silently yelling "help" and getting frustrated that nobody is helping. So we have to ask specifically, such as "I need someone to stain and seal our deck, and since it's a big job, maybe your boys can help too." That's very specific asking. If I do not get a positive answer, I will ask someone else or do it myself, but at least I asked.

Asking is integral to relationships with everyone. Ask your boss if you can take a break. Ask your girlfriend to marry you. Ask your spouse if you can take a trip with your friends. Ask your kids if you can take them to the movies. You have some powerful tools for enriching not only your own life but those around you as well.

Asking is a hallmark of a higher social order. We teach our children to say "please" and "thank you" as common courtesies. This translates into lives of grace, forbearance, and wellbeing. Just take something that belongs to someone else without asking and see what happens to you. Not asking is a good way to land yourself in a lawsuit or jail.

Asking can make us feel humble or embarrassed. If we don't have money to feed our family and have to ask for food stamps or other charity, we might have food, but it can leave us with sticky, uncomfortable feelings.

Like other elements of decency, asking is not always easy, but it is important. Neglecting to ask has its consequences. If we care about other people and about ourselves, we need to ask. Consider the consequences of leaving your job early without asking. That is a simple example of why we should ask. If decency matters to you, ask even when it's hard, even when it's embarrassing, and even when you don't like it.

SAY "THANK YOU" AND BE GRATEFUL!

There are two concepts in this element of decency. One is simply saying the words "thank you." Two is the deeper, more meaningful feeling of gratitude.

We teach our children to say "please" and "thank you." Decency requires us to be polite, but often in our hectic, fast-paced lives, we forget. We need to be reminded to say "thank you" as a part of our daily routine. Sometimes I write things down and post them where I will be sure to see them. If you need a reminder, write the words "thank you" on a sticky note and put it on the dashboard of your car or on the refrigerator door.

Saying "thank you" is an easy way to build and heal relationships. Like an apology, saying "thank you" can take the wind out of a bad situation. Try this in the middle of an argument. Find some reason to say "thank you," and it will stop the argument right there. How can you argue when someone is thanking you?

Gratitude requires a bit more thought. I see and hear people, even children, being mean to each other. They battle through their days, hitting, swearing, and saying horrible things to their siblings, parents, and everyone else. This is a lack of gratitude. We can teach our children to be grateful the same way we teach them to say "please" and "thank you," but not if we don't understand and practice gratitude ourselves.

Right where you are, stop and look around. What do you see? Take a good look. Now close your eyes, get a picture of what you just saw in your mind, and consider those things. Maybe it's your computer, your spouse, or a good book, but wow! You have that. It's yours, and it should fill you with a deep sense of gratitude. Consider what your life would be like without them.

Gratitude brings us happiness. Greater Good: The Science of a Meaningful Life,[6] a website by the University of California, Berkeley, says,

> Research by happiness
> expert Sonja Lyubomirsky, proves

---

[6] Robert Emmons, "Greater Good: The Science of a Meaningful Life," *Benefits of Gratitude* (University of California–Berkeley, November 2010).

that practicing gratitude is one of the most reliable methods for increasing happiness and life satisfaction; it also boosts feelings of optimism, joy, pleasure, enthusiasm, and other positive emotions.

Just watching the act of gratitude can make a positive impression. When I watch a TV commercial and a mother gets a card and breakfast in bed on Mother's Day, the actress cries, but so do I. One simple thank you and one act of gratitude can lift my spirits. If we practice gratitude, we become a shining example for others and have the happiness we deserve.

We have a free, simple, and very powerful way to enrich our own lives and those of everyone around us. Just practice gratitude and say "thank you"! I'm in; how about you?

APOLOGIZE!

"I'm not going to apologize. I didn't do anything wrong!" How many times have you heard this or said it yourself? Apologizing is a touchy subject, but one I include here because, in the name of decency, saying "I'm sorry" needs to be addressed.

Apologizing is much more than saying you were wrong. An apology holds us accountable for our words and actions and gives us a second chance to make something right.

As I have mentioned before, I come from a Catholic background where confession is essential to forgiveness. An apology can heal us and relieve us of heavy burdens. We cannot expect others to forgive us if we cannot confess (which is another way of apologizing).

We apologize for two reasons. First, because we made someone else feel bad. Second, because we ourselves feel bad. We can apologize for hurting someone, and it will make them feel better. But when we apologize, we open ourselves up to forgiveness. Forgiveness is an amazing experience that floods our souls with peace and makes things right again.

I am a big apologizer, even when I don't need to be. I remember my friend Cindy from childhood shaking her head when I would call her to apologize for something I said or did. She always said, "I knew you'd say you were sorry." I believe it is my sensitivity that causes me to believe I hurt others in my words or actions, even when they don't think that. I forget that not everyone is like me. I may go overboard in apologizing, but there are those who never apologize.

I think there can be a middle ground. But in finding that middle ground, there needs to be honesty in communication. We need to pay attention to our words, our tone of voice, and our actions. We need to listen to what others tell us. If we have hurt someone or are hurt because of something we did and need forgiveness, we should hold ourselves accountable and apologize.

As I said earlier, apologizing is a touchy subject. I have heard several people say they shouldn't have to apologize if they offend someone inadvertently. For example, if I post something on Facebook and someone takes offense to it, is it necessary to apologize?

I believe this is up to you. Decide for yourself if it's worth it, but consider the consequences of withholding an apology. The famous feud between the Hatfields and McCoys comes to mind. After the first incident of wrongdoing, there was no apology and no closure. This feud kept up generation after generation, even when nobody remembered what they were feuding about. Someone needed to end that feud. It needed an apology and closure.

Closure begins with an apology, and it is my belief that even a half-hearted apology is better than none at all. The fact that someone thought about the situation and decided to apologize warrants forgiveness. Closure may not be completed at that juncture, but it is a beginning.

I don't know if I have any hard-and-fast rules regarding apologies. That's not what I want to do. I won't judge anyone, but I do believe that decent people will take the high road and just say, "I'm sorry." I wish my mother would have said it.

My mother would never apologize for anything, even if she was confronted with evidence of her error. An example of this took place when I was about eleven years old. Our grandmother, who was visiting our house, told my mother that she was missing some money. My mother called all eight of us into the dining room and interrogated us thoroughly. When nobody confessed, she whipped us all and sent us to bed. The next day, Grandma called, saying she had found the money. My mother told us that Grandma had found the money, and I waited for Mom to apologize for the humiliation and pain she had inflicted. Forty-seven years later, I'm still waiting for an apology, and Mom's been dead for over three of those years.

In the weeks before her death, I asked Mom to think about any regrets or guilt she might be feeling and consider telling people she was sorry. She never did. In her inability and unwillingness to be accountable for her actions, she left this world full of fear because she couldn't say one word, "sorry."

DON'T CHEAT ON A RELATIONSHIP!

There isn't a person alive who isn't devastated when their spouse, girlfriend, boyfriend, etc. cheats on them. It is the height of disrespect and is incredibly hurtful to someone you chose to be involved with on a very intimate level.

Love relationships are complicated, but, at their core, they are chosen. If you can choose to get into a relationship, you can choose to get out of one. A decent person ends one monogamous relationship before starting another.

I have heard it said that love is only for the brave, and I believe that. Love requires commitment, and if you don't want a commitment, it is your responsibility to let someone know that clearly sooner rather than later. If you are not emotionally strong enough to talk to someone openly and honestly, you should not be in a relationship.

Cheating means no sex, no texting, no emails, no phone calls, no flirting, no kissing or other physical contact, and no hanging onto an "ex" for any reason. In legal terms, cheating is a breach of contract if you are married and a breach of ethics if you are in a committed monogamous relationship.

I dated a lot in the fifteen years between my two marriages. I decided early on that it was not worth it for me to be exclusive until I found exactly who I was looking for. I was up front with everyone at the start, and there were some tense moments with some men who could not accept that I wouldn't commit to them. But really, what woman goes into a shoe shop and only tries on one pair?

I don't think it's wrong for someone to date more than one person at a time. However, if you do, you MUST let people know you won't be monogamous. As long as you tell them, it is their decision to go out with you. At least you are honest about it. Cheating is not honest.

Whatever the reason, cheating is wrong, and the only way to make it right is to communicate your intentions. You are not responsible for the response or reaction of someone you are confessing to, but you are responsible for your actions. If I could only use one reference in this book, it is the golden rule. Here it is: DON'T cheat!

TREAT EVERYONE EQUALLY!

Treat your neighbor like the president of the United States, and treat the president of the United States like your neighbor.

I was taught to hate others, and then I was challenged to question my hate by a man I admire and respect. I don't even know who this man is, but I wrote this letter to him to thank him for teaching me not to hate.

Dear sir,

I was born in 1958 in Milwaukee, Wisconsin, and when I was a teenager, I worked at a Shakey's Pizza Parlor on Wisconsin Avenue. You may not remember, but one day, I did something that has haunted me ever since. Let me tell you about it.

Shakey's was having a coupon sale for "Buy One, Get One Free" on any pizza. If someone did not have a coupon, we would give them one. I was taking orders, and I gave a coupon to a man and explained the details to him. But when the next man in line came up to order, I did not tell him about the sale. I did not offer him a coupon. I wasn't even very friendly.

You were that man, and you looked me right in the eye and said, "I want one of those coupons, the one you gave the man in front of me." I immediately felt some slight anger, but there was another element of emotion, and this is the one I don't forget.

The other emotion I felt that day was shame. I felt it then, and I feel it again every time I think about that day. I was a young White teenager, and you were a Black man. I have a vague recollection of you—maybe in your forties and dressed well—but I didn't know you. I have dissected this moment many times over the years, and I realize I behaved like a racist.

I am not a racist now, but at that time in my life, I behaved like one. My father worked in the heating industry and was often in people's homes repairing furnaces. When he came home, he would rant about all of "those" people. If your name was Cuellar, Fonti, or Silverman, he hated you too, but he hated Black people the most. I grew up being afraid of Black people for no other reason than what I heard my father and other adults say about them. But when I was called a "honkey" or a "cracker," I don't think I felt what I think a Black person feels when he or she is called *that* word. You know what it is; my father knew it.

I knew that word because it was bantered around often in those days. It was then, and still is, a horrible word, and I was aware that saying it gave me a sense of power, one I was not used to having in my own home with eight kids and violent parents. But that word also made me afraid. I was afraid of Black people.

My fear stemmed from what I was taught at home, what I saw out in the world and on the news, and what I read. I have always been a voracious reader, and some books tell of Southern slavery: slaves rising up against their owners, killing them, and burning down their homes. In my youth, Black leaders were being lynched, and civil rights activists were being shot. There were riots when Martin Luther King was killed. I was afraid Black people would kill me too. I never thought much about this until the day you asked me why I did not treat you like I treated White customers.

Because you asked me, I did a thorough examination of my motives, my prejudices, and my true beliefs, and I came to the conclusion that I am not a racist. Of course, this did not happen overnight, but it did happen rather quickly. I was raised to hate Black people because my parents were afraid of them. Hate is born of fear. Fear is what I felt. Fear is a very strong emotion and can motivate lots of negativity.

Most people never think about why they hate and never try to get past their fear. We don't reach out in pursuit of understanding or check the reasons why we behave the way we were taught in childhood. Shame on us.

Sir, I am sorry I did not offer you a coupon. I am sorry I behaved the way I did, and I hope you get my apology. That is one hope, but my other hope is that we all stop behaving in racist and otherwise prejudiced ways just because we were taught to. Let's think for ourselves and instead reach out with the hope of understanding the reasons we fear and hate another person we don't even know, just because they look differently than we do.

Thank you for asking me why I did not give you a cou-pon. Thank you for turning me around that day because, in doing so, you gave me the chance to think, question, and change my ways. I no longer fear people because of how they look, so hate is no longer a part of my life.

In grateful sincerity,
Carol Pemrich Hauser

People are becoming more socially sensitive about this, but there is still fear and hate in our country and our world. We need to talk about this together. We need to discuss it and learn who we are on the inside instead of hating each other in fear of who we are on the outside. When I watch the news and see what we are still doing to each other, I cringe. We should be doing more to stop this.

I would like to be a part of open discussions on the subject of prejudged race and other relations, such as gender and sexuality. I know there would be hard conversations filled with fear and the anger that goes hand in hand with being treated badly because of who we are and how we look. I believe we would be giving our world a brighter future if we could overcome fear and hate. It is my opinion that those who have been trampled upon need to forgive those who did the trampling, and, in turn, the oppressors need to be worthy of that forgiveness.

TAKE CARE OF YOURSELF!

Eat well, get enough sleep, and go to the doctor if you are sick. Keep yourself clean, and change your socks and underwear. You know someone who does not take care of themselves. Doesn't that make them hard to be around? How you care for yourself affects everyone around you. There are times when we all feel out of sorts and our own self-care is lacking.

My parents, who could barely take care of themselves, never taught me how to take care of myself, so I had to learn by making every mistake there is. I learned to shower and wear clean clothes by getting disgusted by my own body odor. I learned to go to the doctor when I am sick by getting fired from a job for being absent without a doctor's excuse. I learned to eat healthier by becoming obese and having bariatric surgery. I learned to get mental and emotional help by trying to kill myself and ending up in a mental hospital.

Taking care of myself is something I am learning about even now. In my role as primary caregiver for my husband, who has Alzheimer's disease, I am told all the time to take care of myself. I had no idea how to do that, so I did what I always do: look for books on the subject. I learned many ways to take care of myself in books, and my daughters tease me about my so-called "self-help book" addiction, but I believe we can get better at everything if we learn more and choose to work at it.

We can go overboard with our self-care, though. Some people take hormone injections and go to extravagant spas for extreme treatments for physical health and beauty. I personally draw the line at anal bleaching. We go to gyms, drink green smoothies, and purchase high-tech gadgets to track our very steps as we move through the day. Like Cleopatra in ancient Egypt and Ponce de Leon, we are always trying to find the fountain of youth and beauty.

Taking care of yourself is not only about your body, but your mind, heart, and soul as well. I learned that a good way for me to take care of myself is by writing this book. Writing is a very personal self-care technique for me—it heals my soul. I have been writing since I could pick up a pencil, and I have had lots of poetry and many articles published in my lifetime. I highly recommend it, even if it's just a personal journal. It gets issues out into the air, where they can be dissected, examined, and possibly eliminated.

Taking care of our spiritual health is also important. Delving into who we are, other than our physicality, can lead us to a whole new level of awareness and understanding. Many people turn to religion and a higher power for their spiritual health. Many cultures embrace spiritual practices whose wisdom inspires us to turn inward in our journey through life.

Sometimes we simply cannot take care of ourselves. Maybe we are sick, injured, or in the throes of mental or emotional turmoil. In those times, we need to become especially tuned into our self-respect and ask others for help. In previous chapters, I admitted to having trouble with my personal finances and getting help with day-to-day money and credit management. There is no shame in getting help. There is more shame in continuing to struggle and even failing completely because we are unwilling to ask for help. This is failing to take care of ourselves.

Taking care of ourselves encompasses every single aspect of decency, from being genuine to having the self-respect to ask for help when we need it. If we can become better at taking care of ourselves, we can become much better at helping each other. In the process, we become a world of decent human beings.

ABOUT THE AUTHOR

Carol Pemrich Hauser is a poet who has been published in several media venues. She has been writing since she could pick up a pencil, and she is also a member of the Wisconsin Fellowship of Poets. Carol has a way of drawing readers into her stories, and she enjoys writing just for the enjoyment of it.